Treasures

A Reading/Language Arts Program

Mc Graw Hill **Macmillan McGraw-Hill**

Contributors

Time Magazine, Accelerated Reader

Students with print disabilities may be eligible to obtain an accessible, audio version of the pupil edition of this textbook. Please call Recording for the Blind & Dyslexic at 1-800-221-4792 for complete information.

A

The McGraw·Hill Companies

 Macmillan McGraw-Hill

Published by Macmillan/McGraw-Hill, of McGraw-Hill Education, a division of The McGraw-Hill Companies, Inc., Two Penn Plaza, New York, New York 10121.

Printed in the United States of America

ISBN 0-02-194672-8/1, Bk. 1

2 3 4 5 6 7 8 9 (071/043) 09 08 07

Treasures

A Reading/Language Arts Program

Program Authors

Donald R. Bear
Janice A. Dole
Jana Echevarria
Jan E. Hasbrouck
Scott G. Paris
Timothy Shanahan
Josefina V. Tinajero

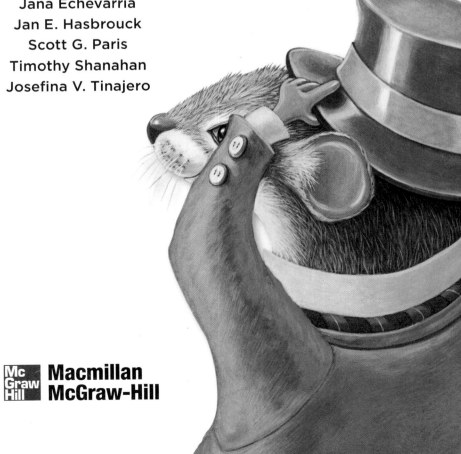

Mc Graw Hill Macmillan McGraw-Hill

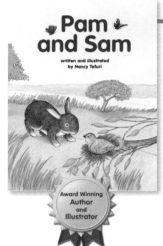

THEME: We Are Special

Talk About It 6

Can Pat Jump? Words to Know 8

Pam and Sam (Fantasy) 14
by Nancy Tafuri

Our Best Days (Social Studies) 28

TCAP Writing: **Personal Narrative** 34

THEME: Ready, Set, Move!

Talk About It 36

Yes, I Can! Words to Know 38

I Can! Can You? (Rhyming Story) 44
by Cathy Roper, illustrated by Lorinda Bryan Cauley

Run! Jump! Swim! (Science) 58

TCAP Writing: **Personal Narrative** 64

THEME: Growing Up

Talk About It 66

I Am a Big Kid Words to Know 68

How You Grew (Nonfiction Article) 70

TCAP **Birds Get Big** (Social Studies) 78

Writing: **Descriptive** 80

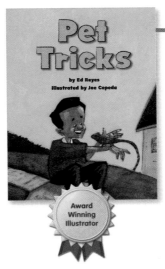

THEME: Pets

Talk About It 82

Come Down, Brad! Words to Know 84

Pet Tricks (Realistic Fiction) 90
by Ed Reyes, illustrated by Joe Cepeda

What Pets Need (Science) 106

TCAP Writing: **Descriptive** 110

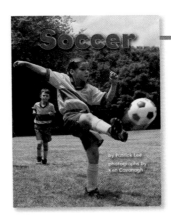

THEME: Teamwork

Talk About It 112

Help for Hank Words to Know 114

Soccer (Nonfiction) 120
by Patrick Lee, photographs by Ken Cavanagh

Guess What! (Poetry) 136
by Michael Strickland

TCAP Writing: **Persuasive** 138

Test Strategy: Right There

Jill and Nat (Realistic Fiction) 140

Glossary 144

We Are Special

Talk About It

What do you like to do? What makes you special?

LOG ON Find out more about being yourself at **www.macmillanmh.com**

jump

up

down

not

P<u>a</u>t

<u>c</u>an

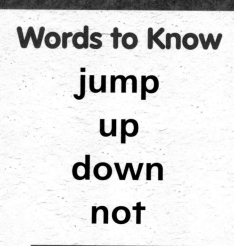

Will Pat jump?

8

Can Pat Jump?

by Ann Carr

illustrated by
Bernard Adnet

Jump up.

Jump **down**.

Pat can **not** jump.

Look! Pat can jump!

Comprehension

Genre

A **Fantasy** is a made-up story that could not really happen.

Story Structure

Character

As you read, use your **Character Chart**.

Pam Can	Sam Can

Read to Find Out

What makes Pam and Sam special?

14

Pam and Sam

written and illustrated
by Nancy Tafuri

Award Winning
Author
and
Illustrator

Pam and Sam like to play.

Pam ran **up**.

Sam ran up.

Pam and Sam ran **down**.

Pam can **jump**.

Sam can **not** jump.

Sam can not go with Pam.

Look at Sam!

Sam can fly.

Go, Pam! Go, Sam!

Say Hello to Nancy Tafuri

Nancy Tafuri says, "I live in the country and love telling stories about animals. I especially like to tell stories about good friends like Pam and Sam. I have fun drawing pictures to go with my stories."

Other books by Nancy Tafuri

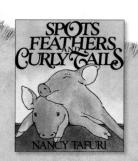

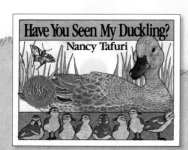

 Find out more about Nancy Tafuri at **www.macmillanmh.com**

 **Write About It**

Nancy Tafuri tells stories about friends. Draw a picture of your friend. Write your friend's name on the picture.

Comprehension Check

Retell the Story

Use the Retelling Cards to retell the story.

Retelling Cards

Think and Compare

Pam Can	Sam Can

1. What can Pam do? What can Sam do?

2. How are Sam and Pam like animals you have seen?

3. How do you know Pam and Sam are good friends?

4. How is Sam like Pat in "Can Pat Jump?"

Our Best Days

Social Studies

Genre
Nonfiction tells about real people and things.

Text Feature
Photographs give more information about the text.

Content Words
neighbor
family
friends

 LOG ON Find out more about what kids like at **www.macmillanmh.com**

What day is the best day?

28

I like Monday.
I ride my horse.

I like Tuesday.
My **neighbor** and I play.

I like Wednesday.
My **family** has pizza.

I like Thursday.
I help my mom plant.

My **friends** and I like Friday.
What is your best day?

Connect and Compare
What might Pam and Sam do on their best day?

Sentence

A **sentence** tells a complete thought.

Write What You Like to Do

Jen wrote a sentence about painting.

I like to paint.

 # Writing Prompt

Think about what
you like to do.

Draw a picture.

Use the sentence frame.

I like to _____.

Writer's Checklist

☑ Did I tell what I like to do?

☑ Does my sentence tell a
complete thought?

☑ Does my sentence begin with a
capital letter?

Ready, Set, Move!

Talk About It

How do you like to move? What can you do?

LOG ON Find out more about movement at **www.macmillanmh.com**

Words to Know

over

it

yes

too

Mac

can

Read to Find Out

What will the pigs do?

STRATEGY SKILL

38

Yes, I Can!

by Alice Tu

illustrated by Diane Greenseid

Can you jump **over it**, Mac?

Yes, I can.

I can, **too**.

We can not!

Comprehension

Genre

In a Rhyming Story, some words end with the same sound.

Story Structure

Sequence

As you read, use your **Sequence Chart.**

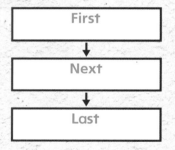

First

↓

Next

↓

Last

Read to Find Out

What will the girl and boy do together?

44

I Can! Can You?

by Cathy Roper

illustrated by Lorinda Bryan Cauley

Award Winning Illustrator

Can you do what I can do?

Yes! I can do **it, too**.

Can you jump **over** a mat?

Can you jump over a hat?

Can you tag a tree?

Can you tag me?

Can you tap, tap, tap?

I can nap, nap, nap.

Can you do what I can do?

Yes! I can do it, too!

Lorinda Bryan Cauley Can, Too!

Lorinda Bryan Cauley says, "I enjoy drawing children jumping, running, and playing. I always try to make each child look different from the others."

Other books by Lorinda Bryan Cauley

 Find out more about Lorinda Bryan Cauley at **www.macmillanmh.com**

Clap Your Hands
Lorinda Bryan Cauley

What Do You Know!
Lorinda Bryan Cauley

Write About It

Lorinda Bryan Cauley draws children playing outside. Draw something you do outside. Label the picture.

Comprehension Check

Retell the Story

Use the Retelling Cards to retell the story.

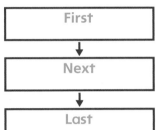

Retelling Cards

Think and Compare

First
↓
Next
↓
Last

1. What do the children do first? Next? Last?

2. What can the children do that you can do, too?

3. What other fun outdoor things can children do together?

4. How is this story like "Yes, I Can!"?

Science

Genre
Nonfiction gives information about a topic.

Text Feature
A **Label** gives information about a picture.

Content Words
helps
move
push

LOG ON Find out more about how animals move at www.macmillanmh.com

Run! Jump! Swim!

What **helps** animals **move**?

back legs

This kangaroo can jump high.
Strong back legs help it jump.

long legs

This cheetah can run fast.
Long legs help it run.

tail

fins

fins

This shark can swim fast.
Its tail and fins **push** it through
the water.

flipper

flippers

This seal is slow on land.
It is fast in the water.
It swims with wide flippers.

Kids can run, jump, and swim, too. What helps kids move?

Connect and Compare
How could animals join the fun in *I Can! Can You?*

Writing

Word Order

The words in a sentence are in an **order** that makes sense.

Write What You Can Do

Tom wrote a sentence about skating.

I can skate.

 **Writing Prompt**

Think about what you can do.

Draw a picture.

Use the sentence frame.

I can _____.

Writer's Checklist

☑ Did I tell what I can do?

☑ Does the order of the words make sense?

☑ Does my sentence end with a special mark?

How have you
changed since
you were little?

 Find out more about
growing up at
www.macmillanmh.com

Growing Up

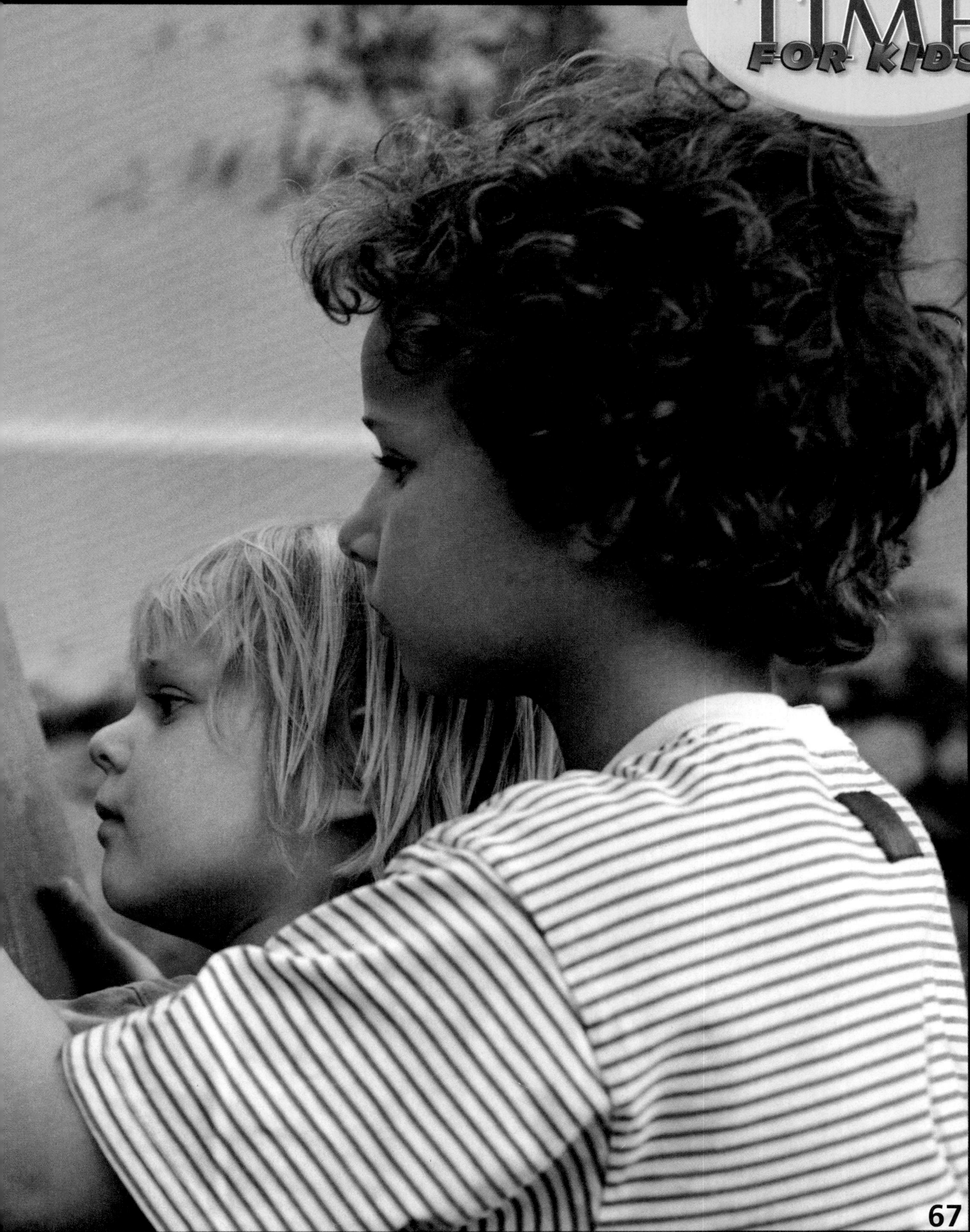

I Am a Big Kid

Words to Know

run

ride

be

big

kid

I am a big kid. What can I do?
I can **run**. I can **ride**.

What can I **be**?
I can be me.

Comprehension

Genre
A Nonfiction Article gives information about a topic.

Text Structure
Sequence
Look for things babies can do. Look for things kids can do as they get older.

How You Grew

How do kids change as they get older?

Once you were little.

You learned to talk. You could say "mama" and "puppy."

You could sit.
You could dig.

You could eat at the table.
You could sing a song.

You learned to **run** and **ride**.
You could go fast.

How big are you now?
How big will you **be**?

 Comprehension Check

Tell What You Learned

Describe what kids learn to do as they get bigger.

Think and Compare

1. What can kids learn to do as they grow older?

2. Name some things you learned before you started school.

3. Name two things babies learn that are not in the story.

4. How are the kids in "I Am a Big Kid" different from the kids in "How You Grew"?

Test Strategy

Right There
You can put your finger on the answer.

READ TOGETHER

Birds Get Big

First, a mother bird lays eggs.

Baby birds grow inside.

Then they hatch.

The mother feeds them.

The babies grow big.

Then they fly away.

Go On ▶

Directions

Answer Numbers 1 to 3.

1 What happens first?

○   ○   ○

2 What happens after the birds hatch?

○ The birds lay eggs.

○ The mother feeds them.

○ The birds make a nest.

Tip
Look for
key words.

3 What happens when the babies are big?

○   ○   ○

STOP ● 79

 **TCAP**

Write About Kids

First Carly drew a picture.
Then she wrote a sentence.

Big kids can ride.

 **Writing Prompt**

Pick something little kids can do.
Think about why they can do it.
Now write a sentence about it.

Writer's Checklist

☑ Does my sentence tell an idea?

☑ Does my sentence begin with a capital letter?

☑ Does my sentence end with a period?

Pets

Talk About It

What pets do you know? What are they like?

LOG ON Find out more about pets at **www.macmillanmh.com**

Words to Know

come
that
on
good

Brad
grab

Read to Find Out
Will Brad come down?

Come Down, Brad!

by Henry Chan

illustrated by Amanda Haley

85

Come down, Brad!

Do not grab **that!**

Jump **on** me.

What a **good** cat you are!

Comprehension

Genre

Realistic Fiction is a made-up story that could really happen.

Story Structure

Setting

As you read, use your **Setting Chart**.

Setting	What the Characters Do There

Read to Find Out

Where do the pets do tricks?

Pet Tricks

by Ed Reyes
illustrated by Joe Cepeda

Come see the pets!

Come see the pet tricks.

Frizz has a **good** trick.

Frizz can jump over a bat.

Ham has a good trick.

Ham can run **on** the track.

Zig has a good trick.

Zig can grab the rope.

Can Kit do a trick?

Kit can not jump over a bat.

Kit will not grab **that** rope.

Kit can kiss!
That is a good trick.

Meet Joe Cepeda's Pets

Joe Cepeda says, "My family likes pets. My son has an iguana, a dog, and a frog. Gizzy, his iguana, goes for walks on a leash! We haven't been able to teach our dog any tricks. I think drawing animals is just like drawing people. They're just fuzzier!"

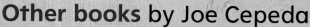

Other books by Joe Cepeda

LOG ON Find out more about Joe Cepeda at **www.macmillanmh.com**

Write About It

Joe Cepeda likes pets. Draw a pet that you like. Label the picture.

Comprehension Check

Retell the Story

Use the Retelling Cards to retell the story.

Retelling Cards

Think and Compare

Setting	What the Characters Do There

1. Where does the story take place?

2. How are the animals in the story like pets you know?

3. What tricks have you seen other pets do?

4. What tricks might Brad from "Come Down, Brad!" do in a pet show?

What Pets Need

Science

Genre
Nonfiction gives information about a topic.

Text Feature
A List is a series of things written in order.

Content Words
need
living things
care

Find out more about pets at
www.macmillanmh.com

What do pets **need**?

Like all **living things**, pets need food.
Some pets eat seeds or plants.

Some pets eat meat or fish.
All pets need fresh water.

Caring for My Rabbit

- Give it food.
- Give it water.
- Change the bedding.
- Brush the fur.

Pets need a safe home.
Pets need our love and **care**.

Connect and Compare
Which pet in *Pet Tricks* would you like?
How would you care for it?

Write About a Pet

Robert wrote about a dog.

Boo is really smart!

Writing Prompt

Think about a pet you know.

Draw a picture.

Write a sentence about the pet.

Writer's Checklist

☑ Will the reader know how I feel?

☑ Does my sentence show strong feeling?

☑ Does my exclamation end with an exclamation mark?

Teamwork

Talk About It

How does a team
work together?

LOG ON Find out more about
teamwork
at **www.macmillanmh.com**

113

Words to Know

help

now

use

very

Hank

hands

STRATEGY SKILL **Read to Find Out**

How will Hank and the girl work together?

Help for Hank

by Linda B. Ross

illustrated by Elivia Savadier

I like to **help** Hank.

I help him dig.

Now I **use** my hands.

It looks **very** good!

Comprehension

Genre

Nonfiction gives information about a topic.

Text Structure

Author's Purpose

As you read, use your **Author's Purpose Chart.**

Clue		Clue

↓ ↓

Author's Purpose

Read to Find Out

Why did the author write *Soccer*?

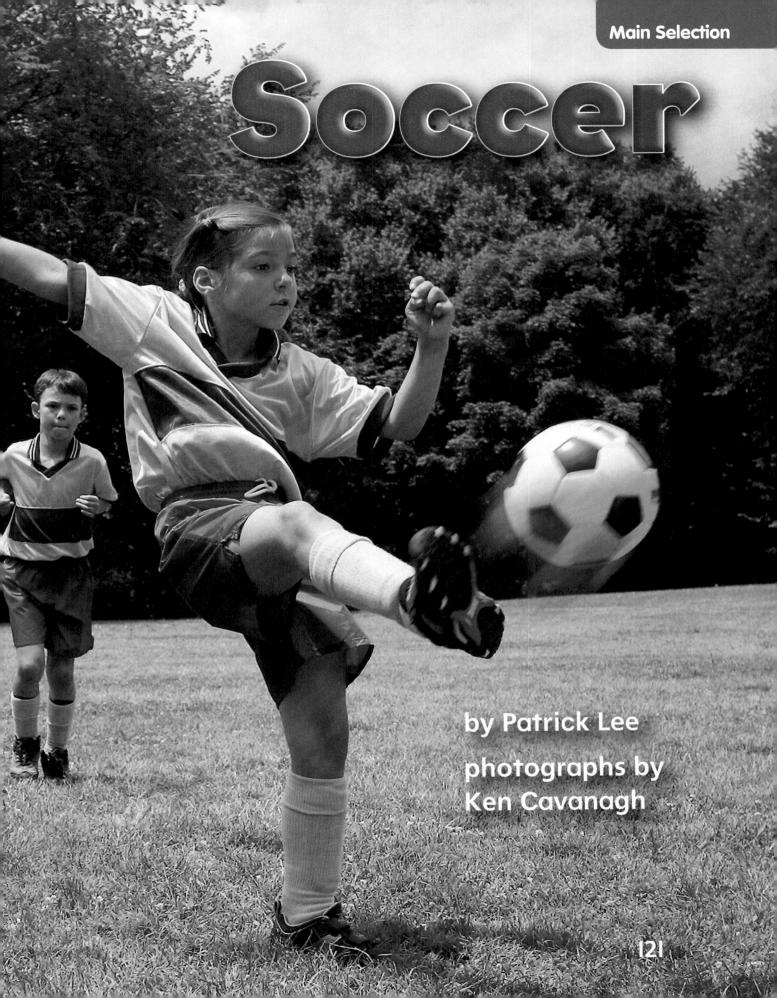

Soccer

by Patrick Lee

photographs by
Ken Cavanagh

We play soccer.

Frank will **help**.
We like Frank.

We run and run.

I run and kick.

I run **very** fast.

I can not **use** my hands.

I kick the ball.
I pass it to Jill.

Now I zig and zag.
I am fast.

I can use my hands.
I am very quick.

Now I grab the ball.

The ball lands in the grass.
It was a very good grab.

Now the game is over.
We like soccer!

Meet the Photographer

Ken Cavanagh says, "Many photographers like to take pictures of one or two things, like sports or family events. I enjoy taking pictures of many things. Besides sports, I like to take pictures of people, places, and nature."

 Find out more about Ken Cavanagh at **www.macmillanmh.com**

 **Write About It**

Ken Cavanagh likes to take pictures of sports. Draw someone playing a sport. Label the picture.

Comprehension Check

Retell the Selection

Use the Retelling Cards to retell the selection.

Retelling Cards

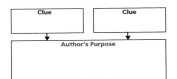

Think and Compare

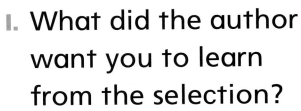

1. What did the author want you to learn from the selection?

2. What games do you like to play? Why do you like them?

3. How do soccer players work as a team?

4. How does the soccer team use teamwork like Hank and the girl in "Help for Hank"?

Poetry

Genre
In a **Poem**, words often rhyme.

SKILL ✓
Literary Element
Words that **Rhyme** end with the same sound.

LOG ON Find out more about teamwork at **www.macmillanmh.com**

READ TOGETHER

Guess What!

by Michael R. Strickland

Black and white
Kicked with might

Smooth and round
Air bound

Passed and rolled
Toward the goal

Rise and fall
A soccer ball.

Connect and Compare
What do both *Soccer* and "Guess What!"
tell about how to play soccer?

Writing

Writing Sentences

A **sentence** begins with a capital letter and ends with a special mark.

Write About a Sport

Pat wrote about baseball.

Baseball is the best sport.
I like to hit the ball.

Writing Prompt

Pick your favorite team sport.
Think about why you like it.
Write about why it is
the best sport.

Writer's Checklist

☑ Did I tell why I like the sport?

☑ Does each sentence tell a
complete thought?

☑ Does each sentence begin with
a capital letter?

Jill and Nat

TCAP **Test Strategy**

Right There
The answer is right there on the page.

Jill is six.

She likes to dig.

She plays in the sand.

Go On ▶

Nat is six, too.

He likes to ride.

He can go up the hill.

Answer Questions

Tip

Look for the answer on the page.

Directions

Answer Numbers 1 to 3.

1 What does Jill like to do?

○   ○   ○

2 What does Nat like to do?

○   ○   ○

3 Where can Nat ride?

○ up the hill

○ in the sand

○ in the house

TCAP Writing Prompt

Write about yourself.
Tell what you like to do.
Write two sentences.

Glossary

What is a Glossary?

A glossary can help you find the meanings of words. The words are listed in alphabetical order. You can look up a word and read it in a sentence. There is a picture to help you.

Sample Entry

Letter

M m

Main Entry

Sentence

mat

I wipe my feet on the **mat.**

Bb

bat

I hit the ball with my **bat**.

Dd

dig

We can **dig** in the sand.

Ff

fast

I run **fast**.

fly

Birds **fly** in the sky.

Gg

grab

Grab the kitten before it gets away.

Hh

hat

The boy has a red **hat**.

help

Amy gets **help** from her dad.

Mm

mat

I wipe my feet on the **mat.**

Nn

nap

Jill takes a **nap** on the couch.

Pp

pet

I love my **pet** dog.

Rr

ride

I go for a **ride** on my bike.

Tt

track

My truck can go on the **track**.

Acknowledgments

The publisher gratefully acknowledges permission to reprint the following copyrighted material:

"Guess What!" by Michael Strickland © 2000, Harper Collins, Reprinted with permission of Harper Collins, NY

Book Cover, CLAP YOUR HANDS by Lorinda Bryan Cauley. Copyright © 1997 by Lorinda Bryan Cauley. Reprinted by permission of G. P. Putnam's Sons, a division of Penguin Putnam Books for Young Readers.

Book Cover, HAVE YOU SEEN MY DUCKLING? by Nancy Tafuri. Copyright © 1996 by Nancy Tafuri. Reprinted by permission of Greenwillow Books.

Book Cover, MICE AND BEANS by Pam Munoz Ryan, illustrated by Joe Cepeda. Text copyright © 2001 by Pam Munoz Ryan. Illustrations copyright © 2001 by Joe Cepeda. Reprinted by permission of Scholastic Inc.

Book Cover, SPOTS FEATHERS AND CURLY TAILS by Nancy Tafuri. Copyright © 1988 by Nancy Tafuri. Reprinted by permission of Greenwillow Books.

Book Cover, VROOMALOOM ZOOM by John Coy, illustrated by Joe Cepeda. Text copyright © 2002 by John Coy. Illustrations copyright © 2002 by Joe Cepeda. Reprinted by permission of Dragonfly Books.

Book Cover, WHAT DO YOU KNOW! by Lorinda Bryan Cauley. Copyright © 2001 by Lorinda Bryan Cauley. Reprinted by permission of G. P. Putnam's Sons, a division of Penguin Putnam Books for Young Readers.

ILLUSTRATION
Cover Illustration: Mary Jane Begin

8-13: Bernard Adnet. 14-25: Nancy Tafuri. 28-33: Eileen Hine. 34: (c) Diane Paterson. 38-43: Diane Greenseid. 44-55: Lorinda Bryan Cauley. 84-89: Amanda Haley. 90-103: Joe Cepeda. 114-119: Elivia Savadier. 122-133: Jon Nez. 136-137: (bkgd) Cheryl Mendenhall. 138: (c) Diane Paterson. 140-143: Benton Mahan. 144-151: Carol Koeller.

PHOTOGRAPHY
All Photographs are by Macmillan/McGraw Hill (MMH) except as noted below:

6-7: BananaStock/Alamy. 7: (tr) Comstock. 26: (tr) Courtesy Nancy Tafuri. 29: (c) Andersen Ross/Brand X Pictures/Getty Images, Inc. 30: (c) Image Source/Alamy. 31: (c) Brand X Pictures/Alamy. 32: (c) SW Productions/Brand X Pictures/Alamy. 33: (c) Tom & Dee Ann McCarthy/CORBIS. 34: (c) Dynamic Graphics Group/Creatas/Alamy. 35: (c) C SQUARED STUDIOS/Getty Images, Inc. 36-37: Ariel Skelley/CORBIS. 37: (tr) Ryan McVay/Getty Images, Inc. 56: (tr) Courtesy Lorinda Bryan Cauley. 58: (c) Mike Hill/AGE Fotostock. 59: (c) Medford Taylor/National Geographic Image Collection. 60: (c) Tom Brakefield/CORBIS. 61: (c) Jeffrey L. Rotman/CORBIS. 62: (l) David Madison/Stone/Getty Images, Inc.; (r) Peter Scoones/Taxi/Getty Images, Inc. 63: (c) Bob Gomel/CORBIS. 64: (c) COMSTOCK. 65: (t) Ingram Publishing/Alamy. 66-67: Kevin Fitzgerald/Stone/Getty Images, Inc. 68: (c) C Squared Studios/Photodisc/Getty Images, Inc. (inset) David Stoecklein/CORBIS. 69: (c) Lawrence Migdale. 70: (bc) Janis Christie/Photodisc/Getty Images, Inc. 71: (tc) Skip Nall/Photodisc/Getty Images, Inc. 72: (tc) Blaine Harrington, III; (bc) Elyse Lewin/CORBIS. 73: (c) Lawrence Migdale. 74: (tl) Don Smetzer/Photo Edit Inc.; (c) Cheryl Clegg/Index Stock Imagery. 75: (tl) Myrleen Ferguson Cate/Photo Edit Inc.; (c) David Muscroft/SuperStock. 76: (c) Nick Clements/Photodisc/Getty Images, Inc. 78: (cr) Darren Bennett/Animals Animals. 79: (tl) Darren Bennett/Animals Animals; (tc) McDonald Wildlife Photography/Animals Animals; (tr) Don Enger/Animals Animals; (bl) Michael Habicht/Animals Animals; (bc) Michael Habicht/Animals Animals; (br) McDonald Wildlife Photography/Animals Animals. 80: (tcr) Maria Taglienti-Molinari/Brand X Pictures/Punchstock. 81: (c) Dian Lofton for TFK; (tcr) Dian Lofton for TFK; (bcr) C Squared Studios/Photodisc/Getty Images, Inc. 82-83: Timothy Shonnard/Getty Images, Inc. 83: (tr) G.K. & Vikki Hart/Getty Images, Inc. 104: (tr) Susan Werner. 106: Gabe Palmer/CORBIS. 107: (l) Richard Hutchings/Photo Edit Inc.; (r) Robert Maier/Animals Animals/Earth Scenes. 108: (c) PhotoStockFile/Alamy. 109: (c) Steve Satushek/The Image Bank/Getty Images, Inc. 110: (c) Diane Paterson; (c) Kevin Radford/Masterfile. 111: (tr) Bildagentur Franz Waldhaeusl/Alamy; (inset) Yiap/AGE Fotostock. 112-113: Image 100/Alamy. 113: (tr) Royalty-Free/CORBIS. 138: (t) Duomo/CORBIS. 139: (c) C Squared Studios/Getty Images, Inc. 145: (t) Stephen Wisbauer/Botonica/Getty Images. 146: (t) Jules Frazier/Getty Images, Inc. 147: (t) Norbert Schaefer/CORBIS; (b) Steve Hamblin/Alamy. 148: (b) Digital Vision Direct. 149: (b) Stephen Wisbauer/Botonica/Getty Images. 150: (b) Michael Keller/CORBIS. 151: (t) Photodisc Red/Getty Images.

Special thanks to Carlos C. Oliveria and the Soccer Academy, New York, New York.